Nola the Nurse®

Math Worksheets for First Graders

Volume 6

by Dr. Scharmaine L. Baker NP

Illustrated by Marvin Alonso

New Orleans, Louisiana

COPYRIGHT ©2016 by Dr. Scharmaine L. Baker and its licensors.
All rights reserved.

No part of this book may be reproduced or transmitted in any form or by any means, electronic or mechanical, including photocopy, recording, or by any information storage and retrieval system without the written permission of the publisher or author except where permitted by law.

For information address A DrNurse Publishing House
2475 Canal Street, Suite 105, New Orleans, La. 70119
www.NolatheNurse.com

ISBN-13: 978-1-945088-10-0
ISBN-10: 1-945088-10-0

Author Contact info:
DrBakerNP@NolaTheNurse.com

www.DrBakerNP.com
www.NolaTheNurse.com

GRADE 1 — ADDITION BOOK — MATHS

COUNT THE NUMBERS
CUT AND PASTE ACTIVITIES

www.nolathenurse.com

COUNT & WRITE THE NUMBERS 1 TO 10

Name : -

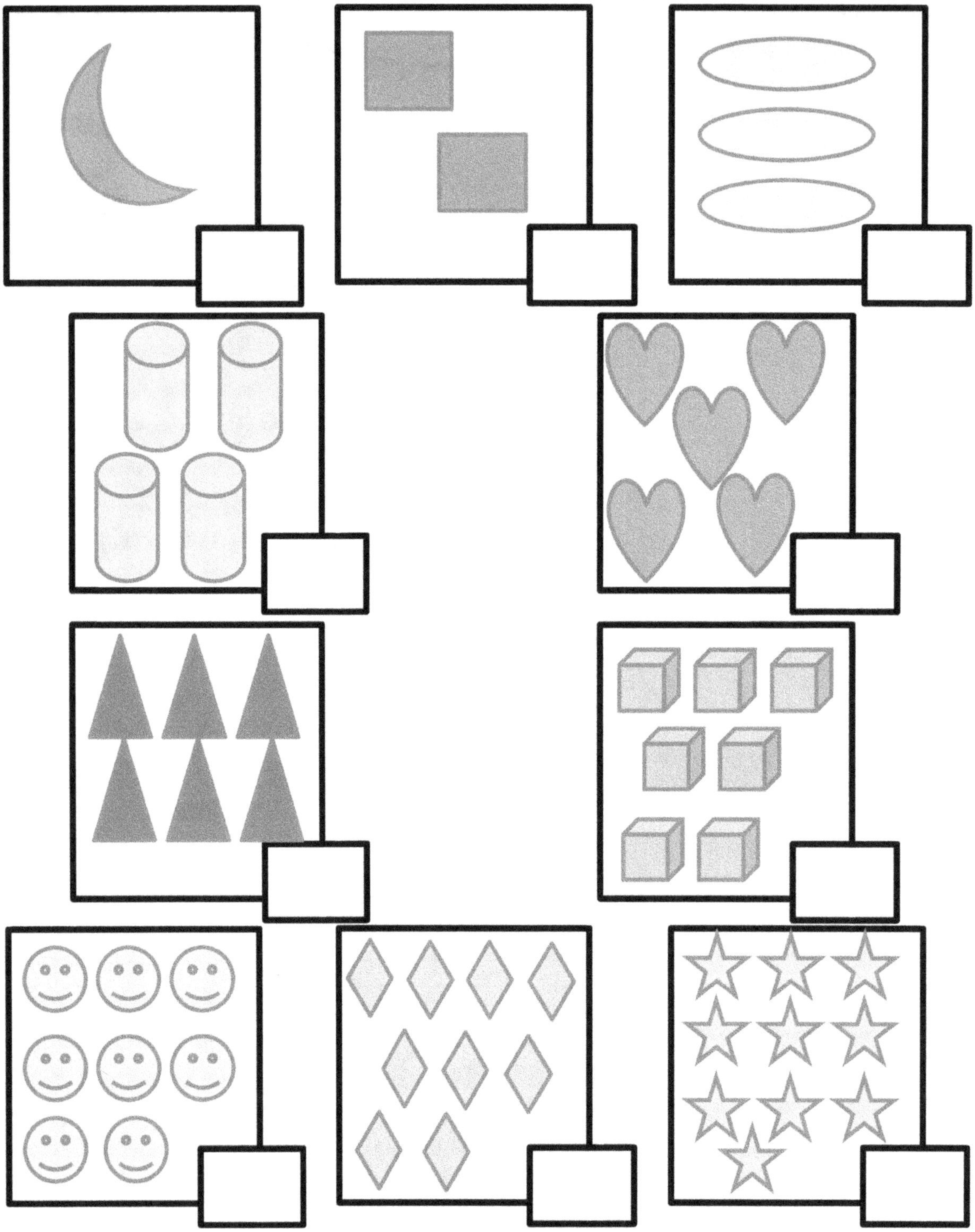

NUMBERS

COUNT & PASTE THE CORRECT NUMBER

www.nolathenurse.com

NUMBERS

COUNT & PASTE THE CORRECT NUMBER

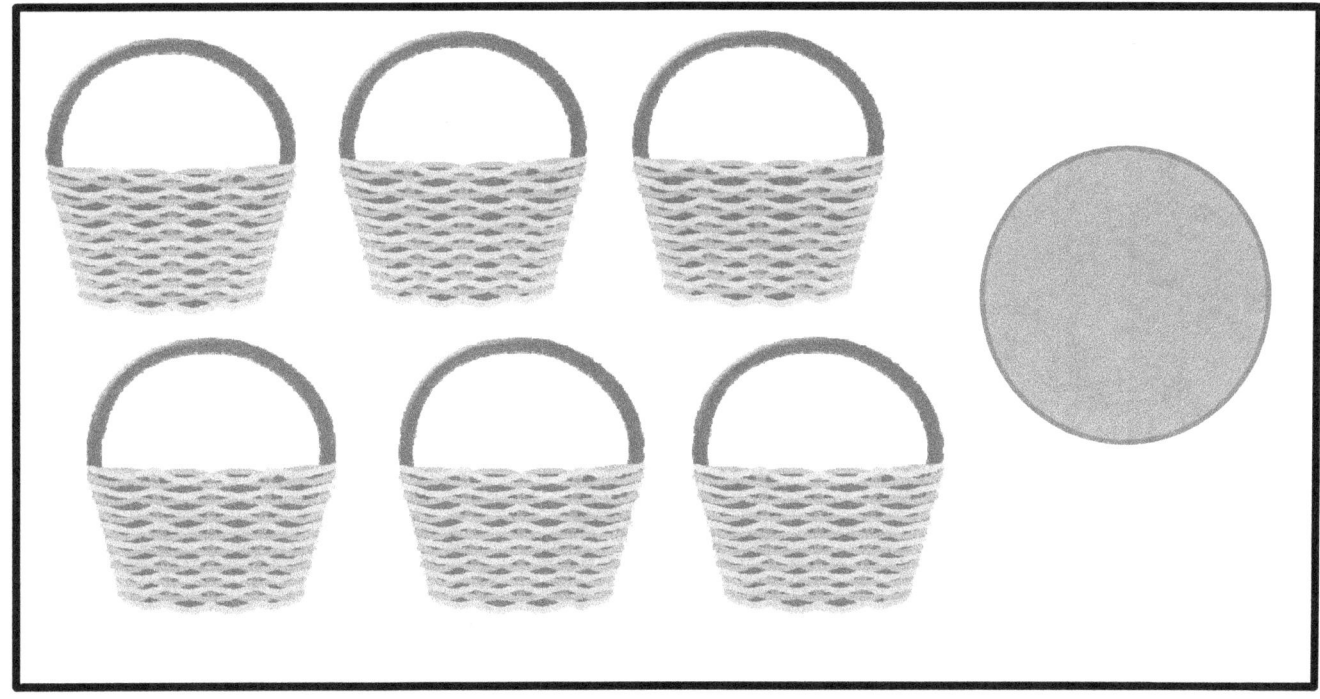

www.nolathenurse.com

NUMBERS

COUNT & PASTE THE CORRECT NUMBER

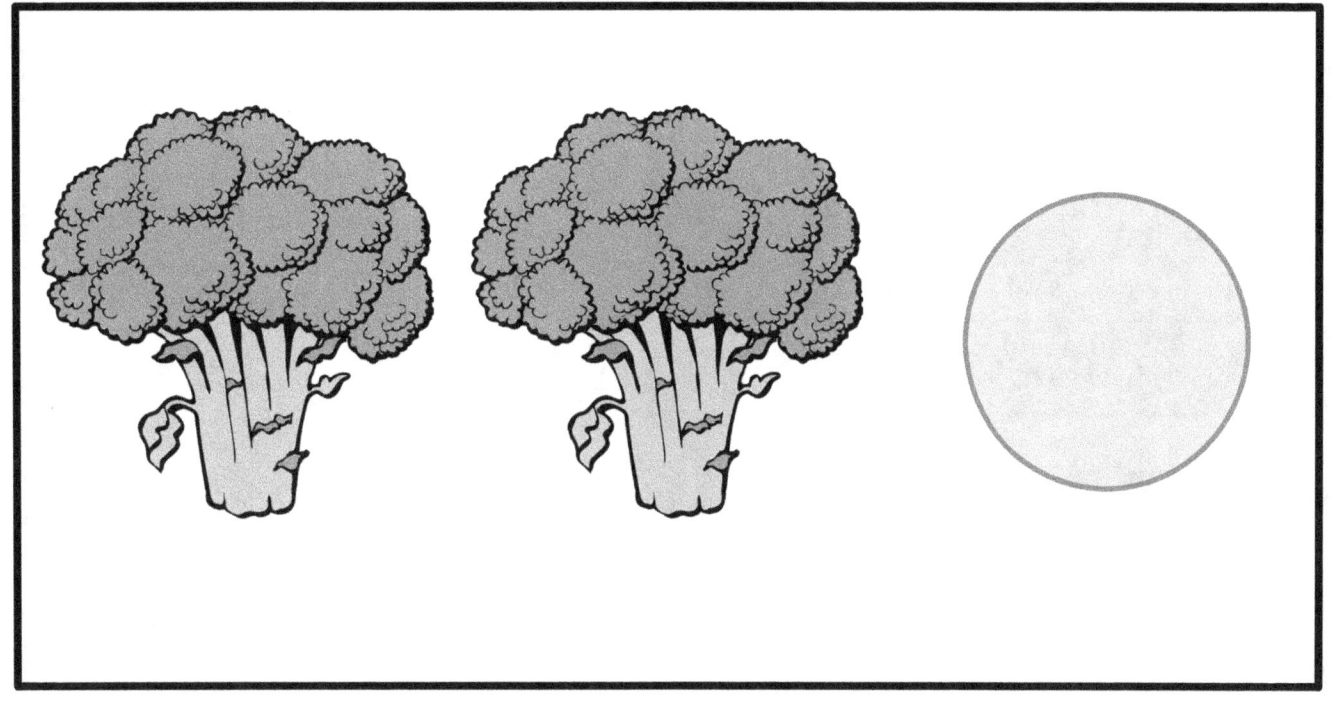

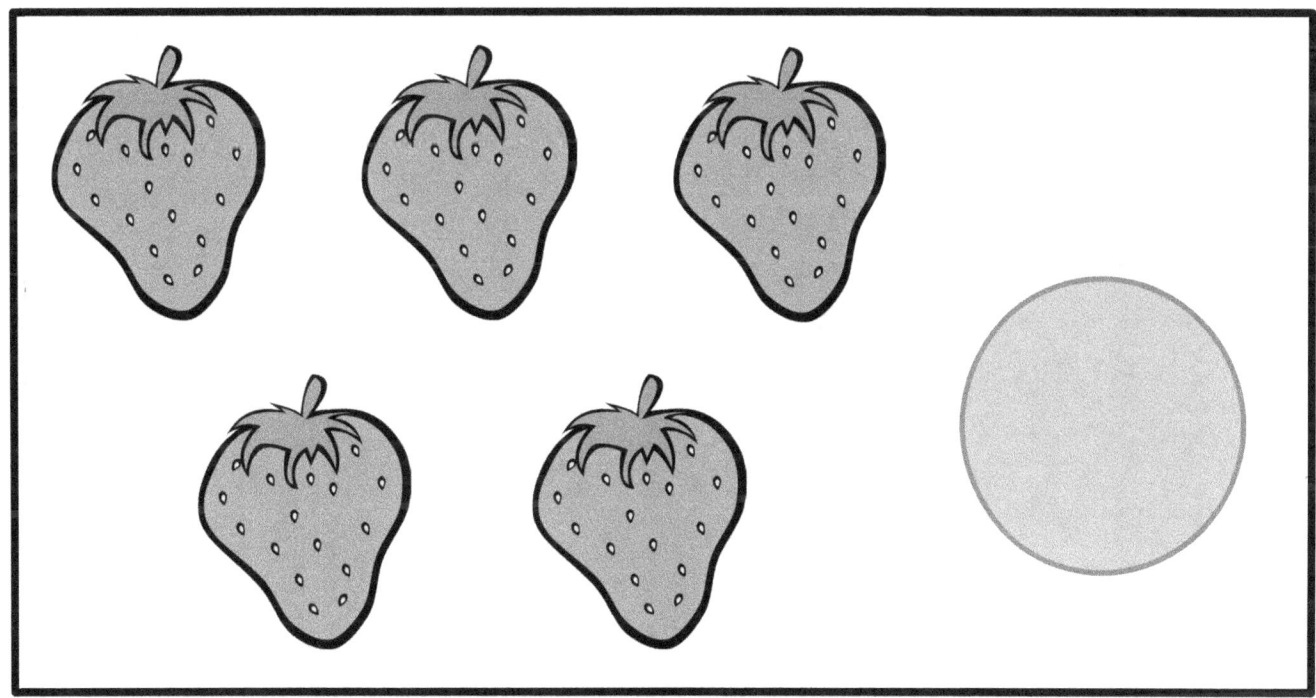

NUMBERS

PASTE 4 MORE PIGGIES TO COMPLETE 10.

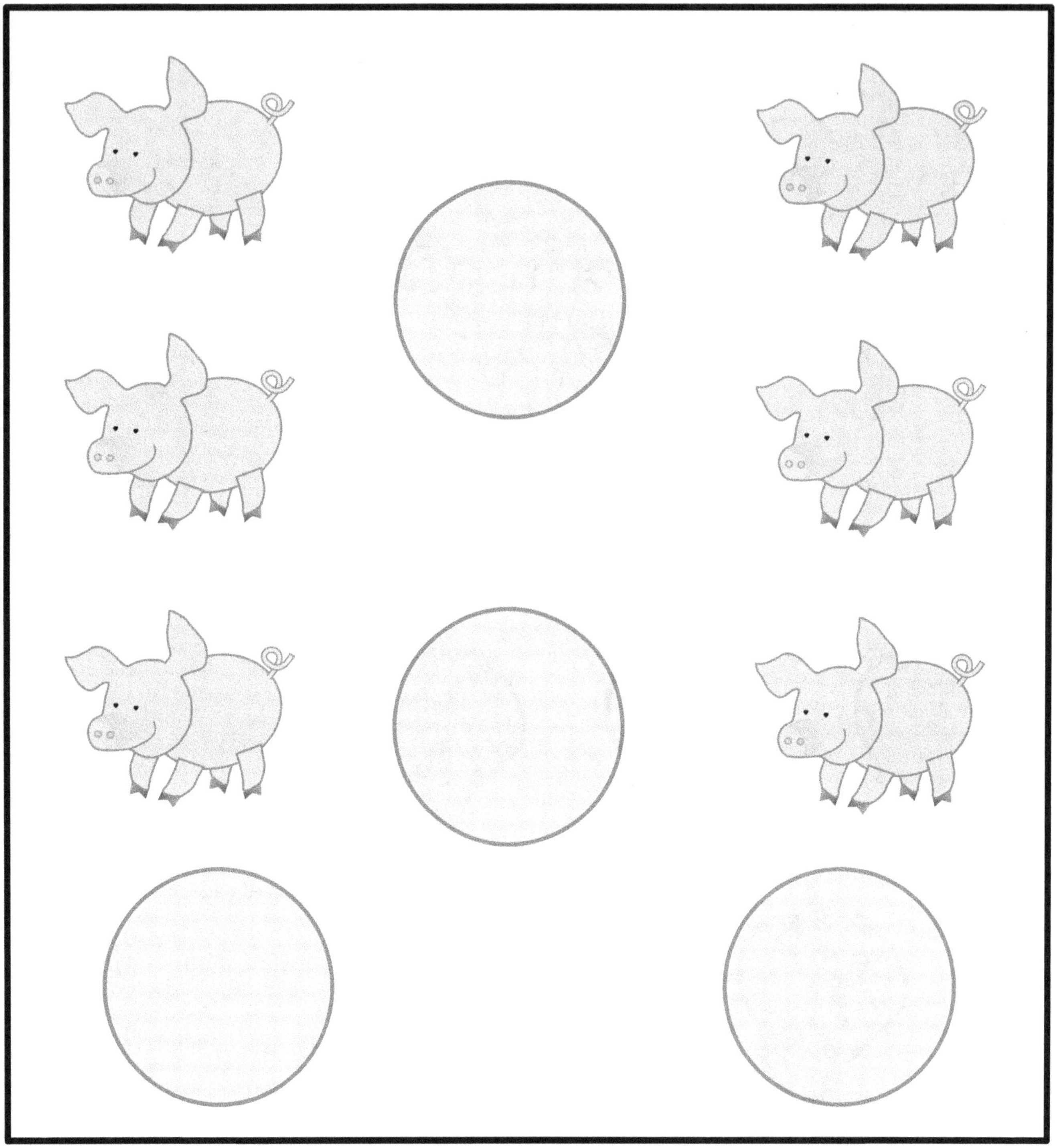

www.nolathenurse.com

NUMBERS 1 to 5

FIND & PASTE THE CORRECT NUMBER OF DOTS.

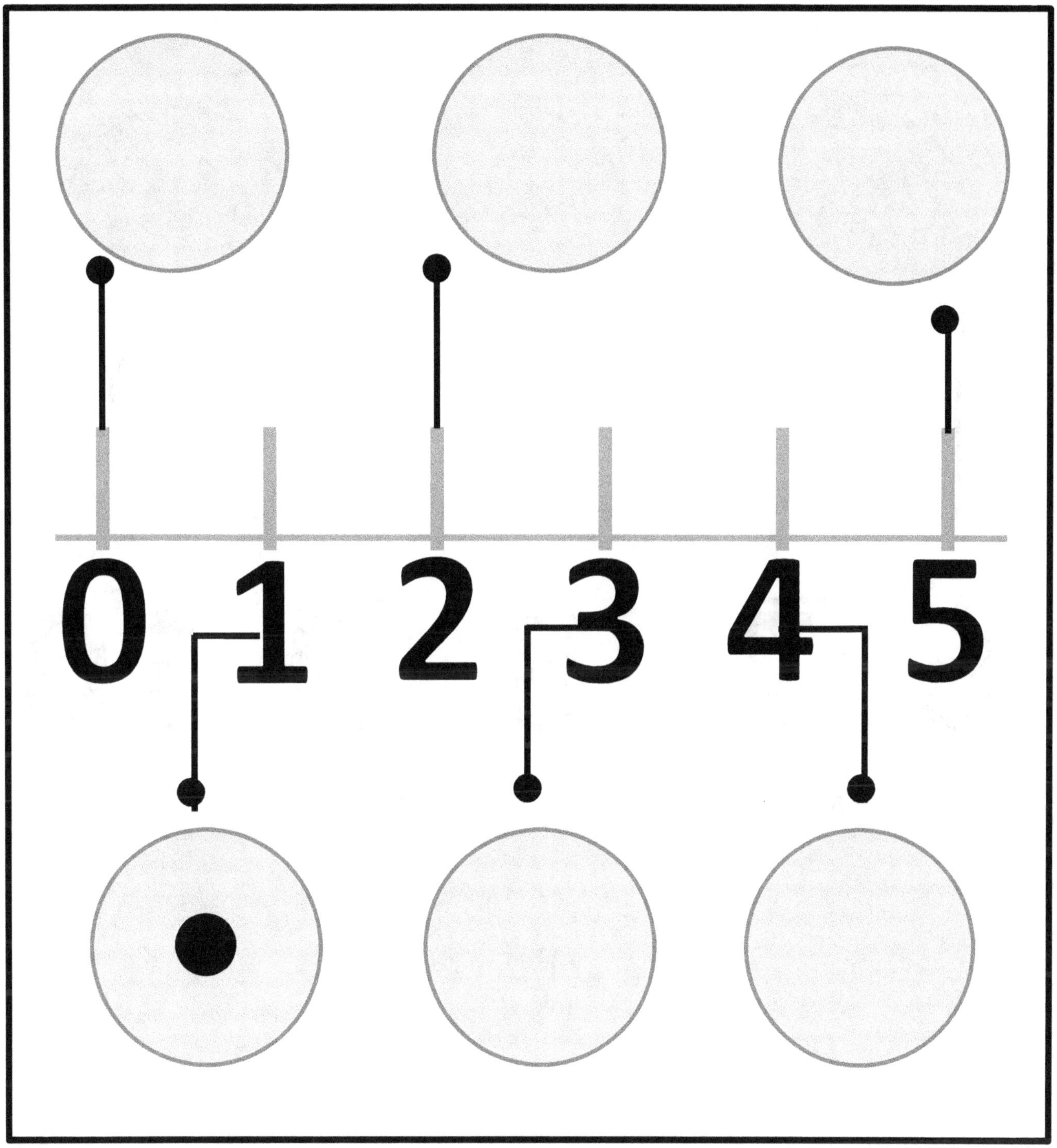

www.nolathenurse.com

NUMBERS 6 to 10

FIND & PASTE THE CORRECT NUMBER OF DOTS.

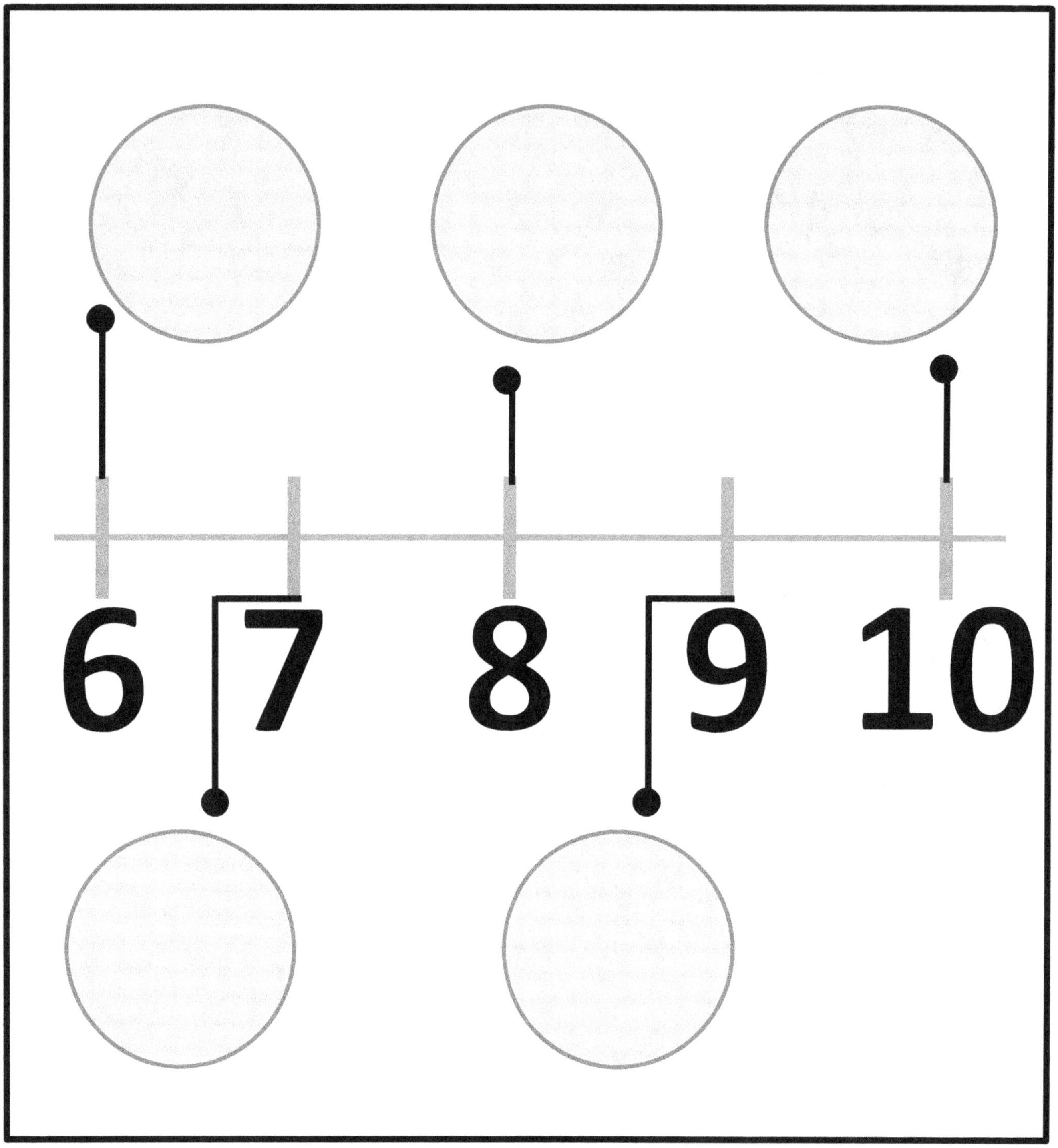

6 7 8 9 10

www.nolathenurse.com

NUMBERS

COUNT & PASTE THE CORRECT NUMBER

NUMBERS

COUNT & PASTE THE CORRECT NUMBER

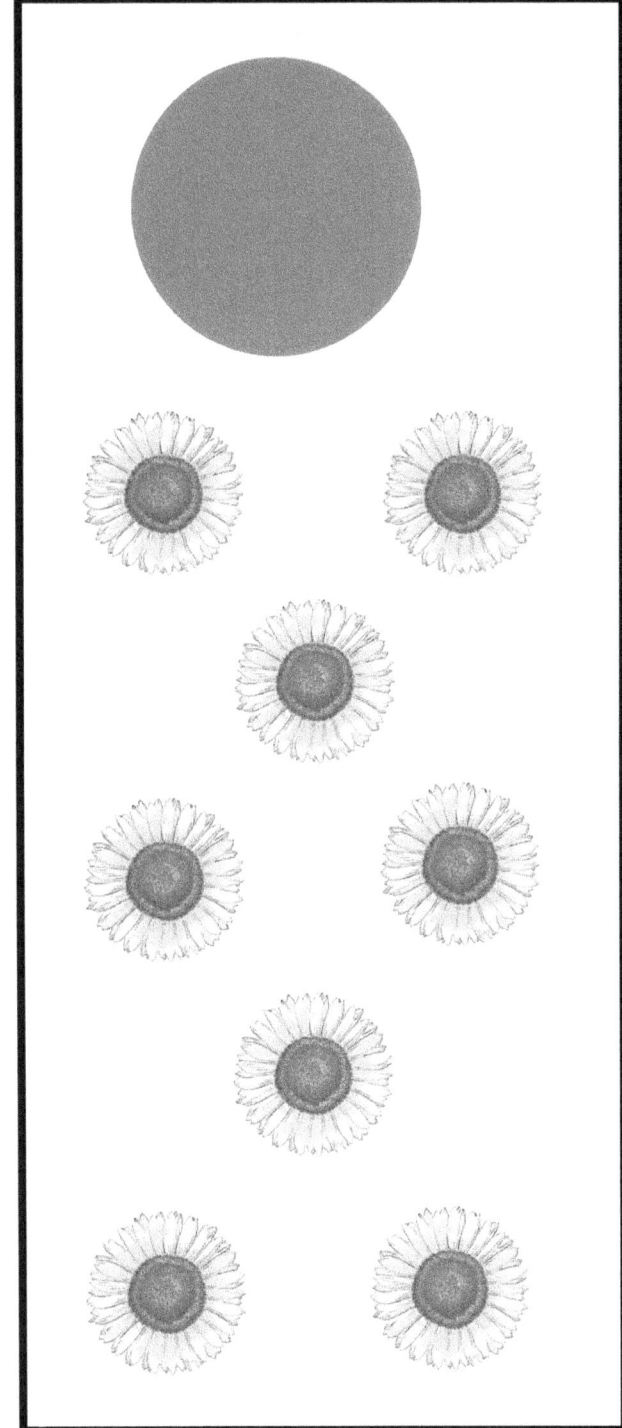
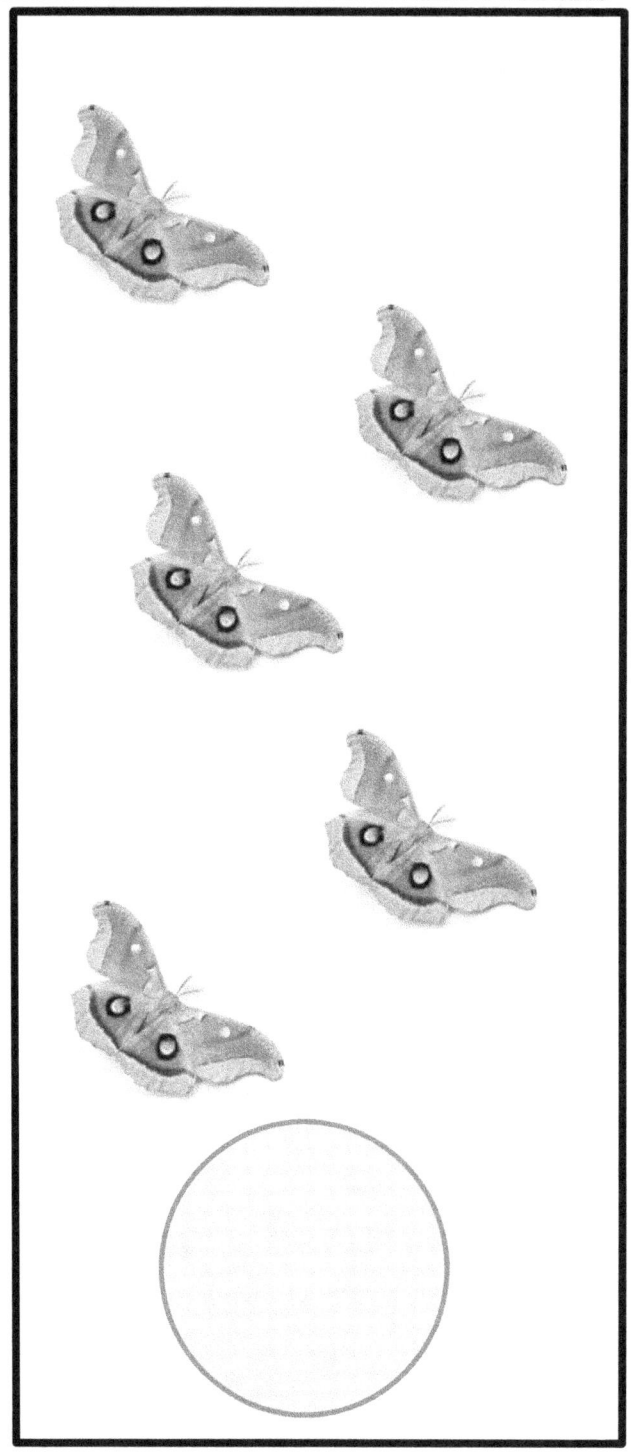

ADDITION OF 1

ADD ONE TO EACH GROUP.

2 + 1

= ___ caps

www.nolathenurse.com

ADDITION OF 1

ADD ONE TO EACH GROUP.

+

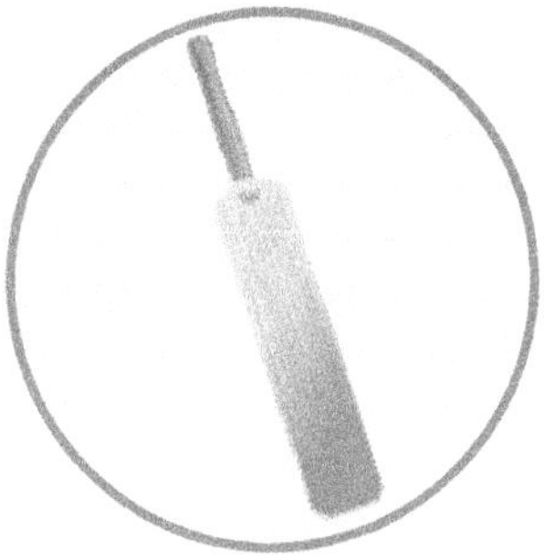

◯ + 1

= ◯ bats

ADDITION OF 1

ADD ONE TO EACH GROUP.

🐟 🐟   +   ⬤
🐟 🐟

⬤   +   ①

= ◯ fishes

www.nolathenurse.com

ADDITION OF 1

ADD ONE TO EACH GROUP.

🐜 🐜
🐜   +
🐜 🐜

                +   1

= ◯   ants

www.nolathenurse.com

ADDITION OF 1

ADD ONE TO EACH GROUP.

🥭🥭🥭
🥭🥭🥭 + ⃝

◯ + ①

= ◯ mangoes

ADDITION OF 1

ADD ONE TO EACH GROUP.

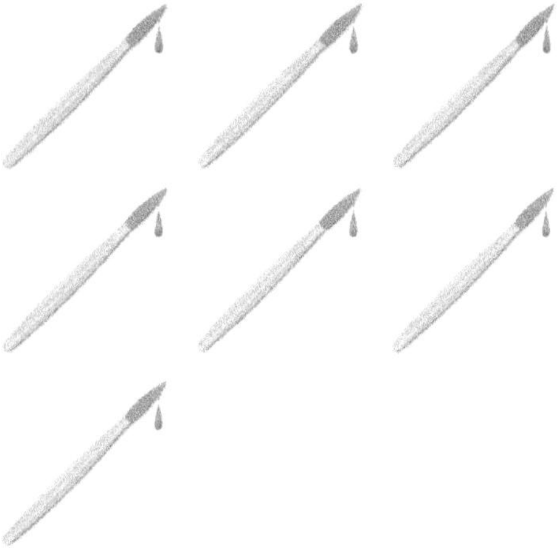

+

+ 1

= ◯ brushes

www.nolathenurse.com

ADDITION OF 1

ADD ONE TO EACH GROUP.

□ + 1

= ◯ rams

ADDITION OF 1

ADD ONE TO EACH GROUP.

🌂🌂🌂🌂
🌂🌂🌂   +   ◯
🌂🌂

◯   +   ①

= ◯ umbrellas

www.nolathenurse.com

ADDITION OF 2

ADD TWO TO EACH GROUP.

🚀🚀 + 🚀🚀

2 + 2

= 4 rockets

www.nolathenurse.com

ADDITION OF 2

ADD TWO TO EACH GROUP.

🏏🏏🏏 + ⃝

⃝ + ⃝

= ⃝ bats

ADDITION OF 2

ADD TWO TO EACH GROUP.

🐟🐟
🐟   +   ◯
🐟🐟

◯   +   ②

= ◯ fishes

www.nolathenurse.com

ADDITION OF 2

ADD TWO TO EACH GROUP.

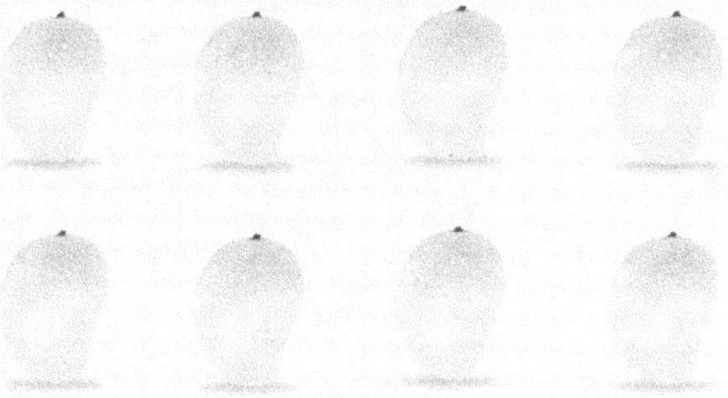

8 🥭 + ⬚

⬚ + 2

= ⬚ mangoes

ADDITION

COUNT AND ADD

→ Example

1 + 2 = 3

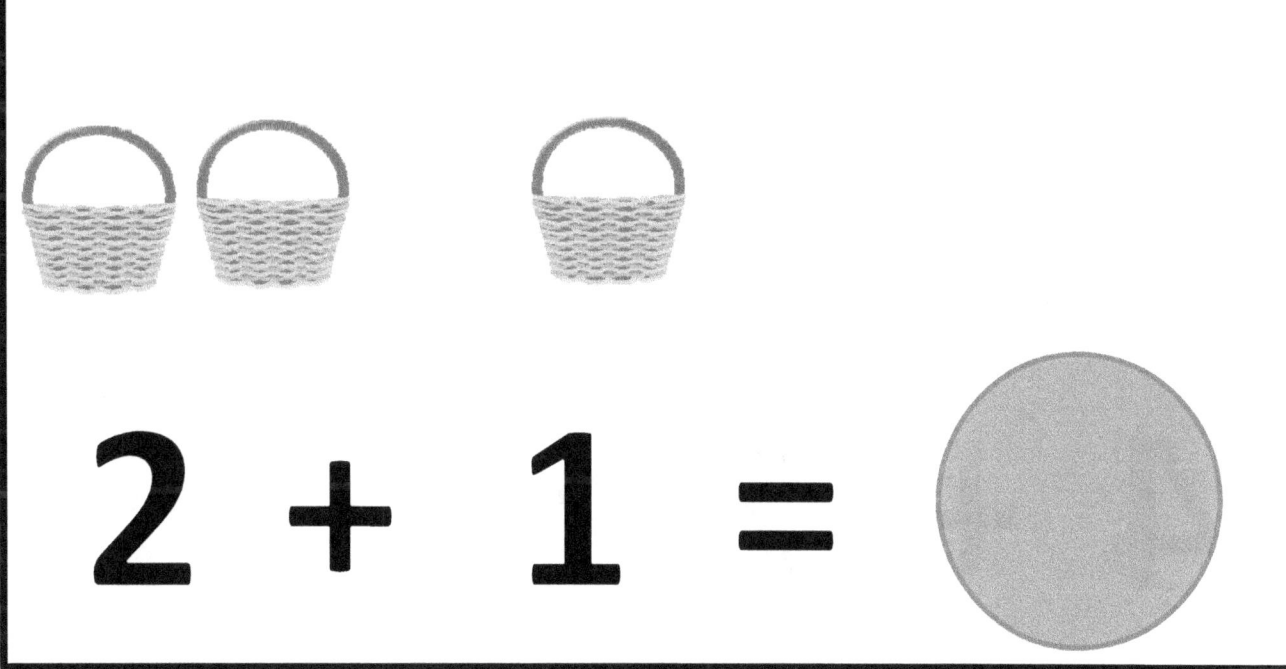

2 + 1 =

www.nolathenurse.com

ADDITION

COUNT AND ADD

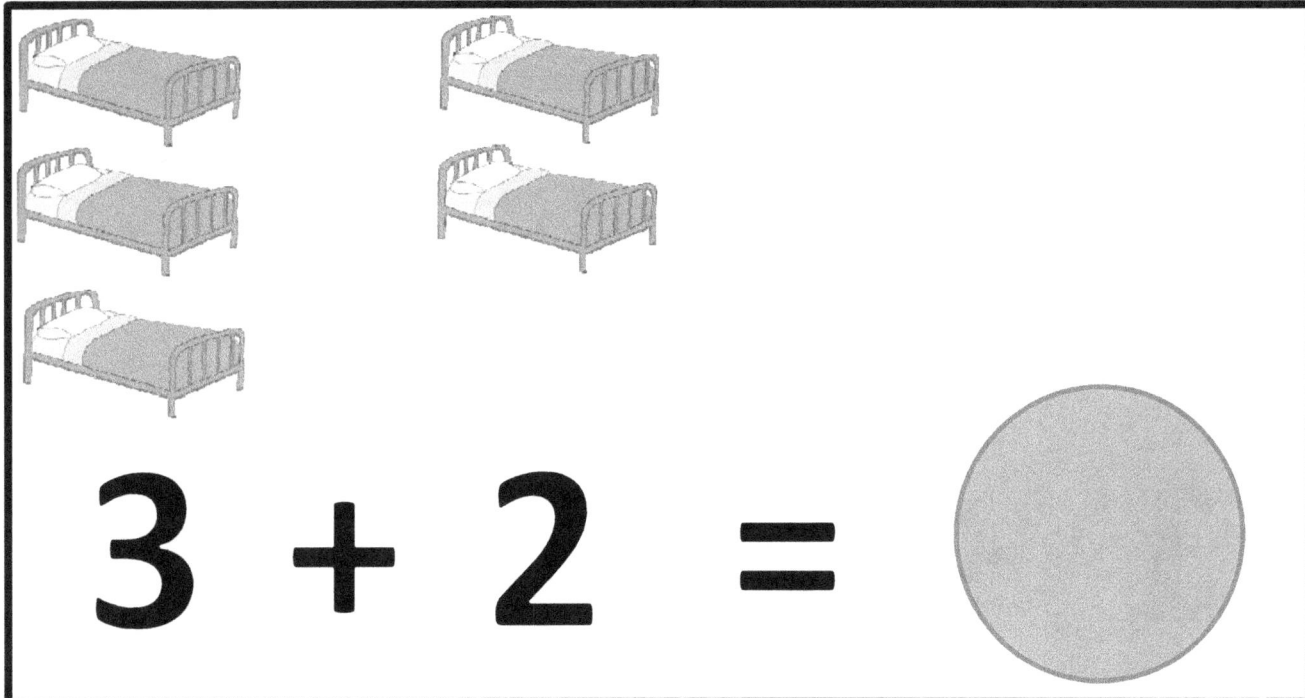

ADDITION

COUNT AND ADD

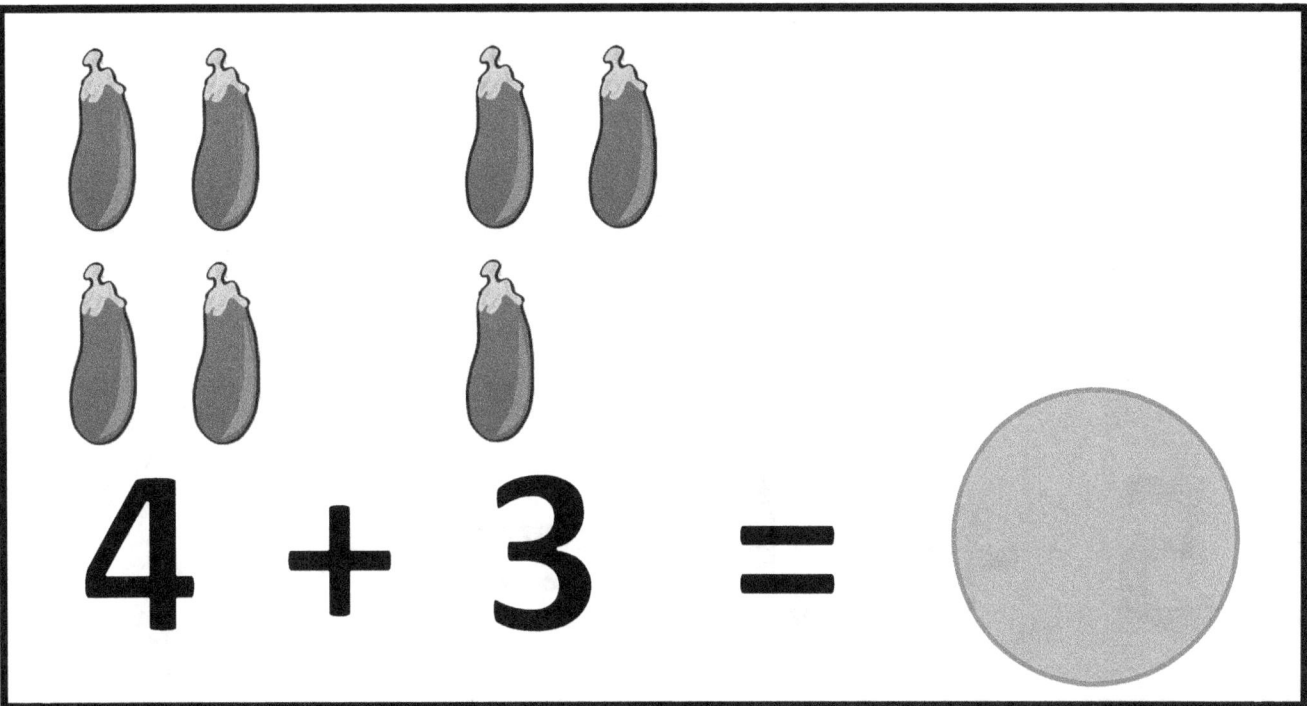

4 + 3 =

6 + 2 =

Make 6

ADD TO MAKE 6 IN EACH GROUP.

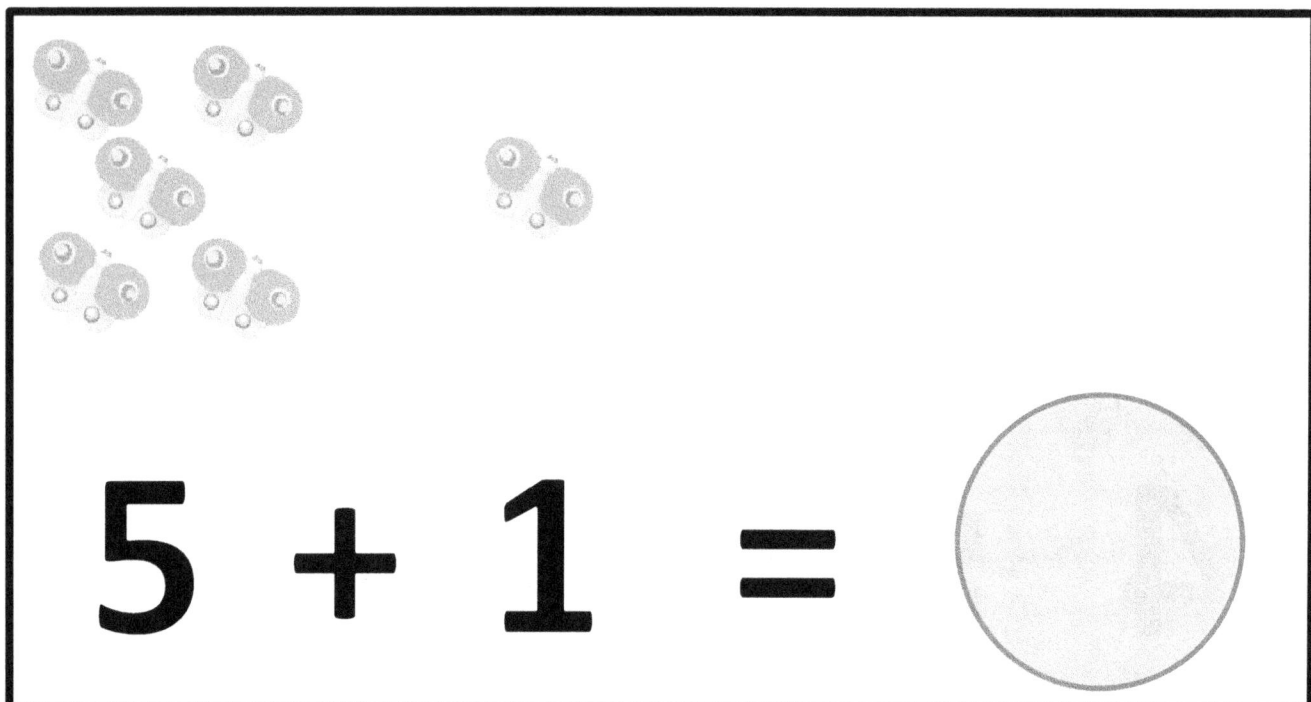

5 + 1 =

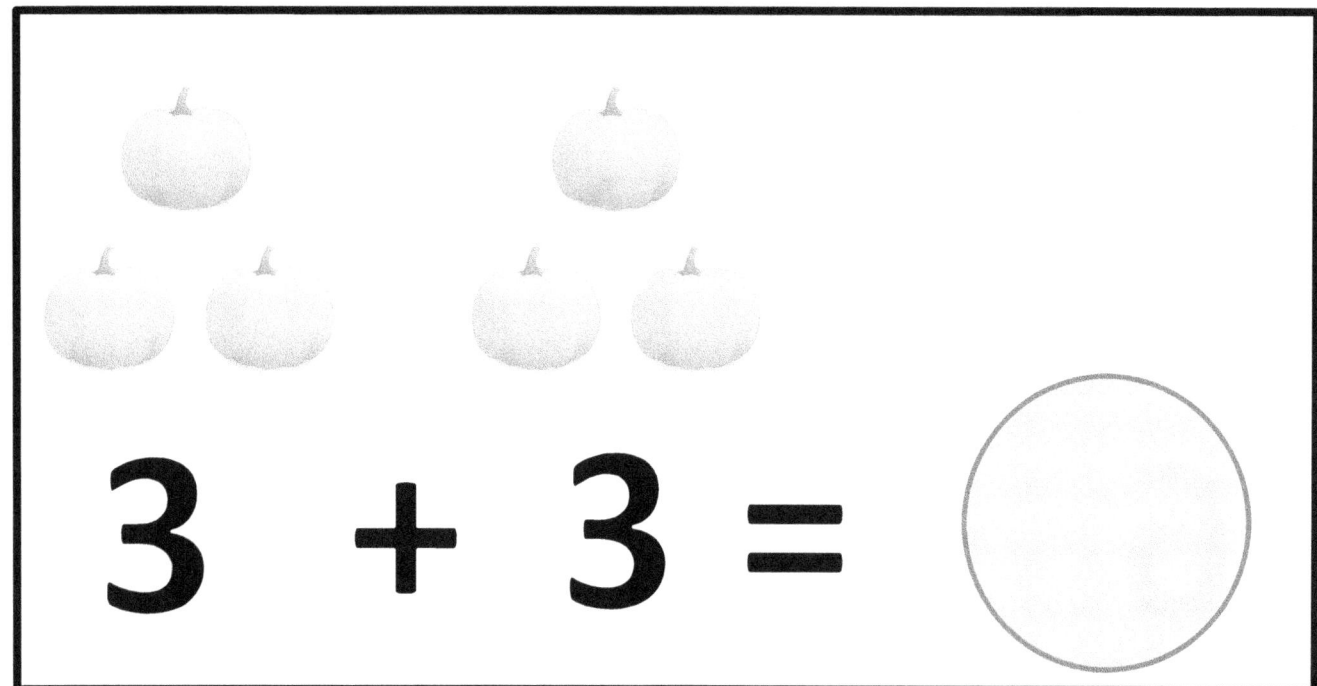

3 + 3 =

Make 6

ADD TO MAKE 6 IN EACH GROUP.

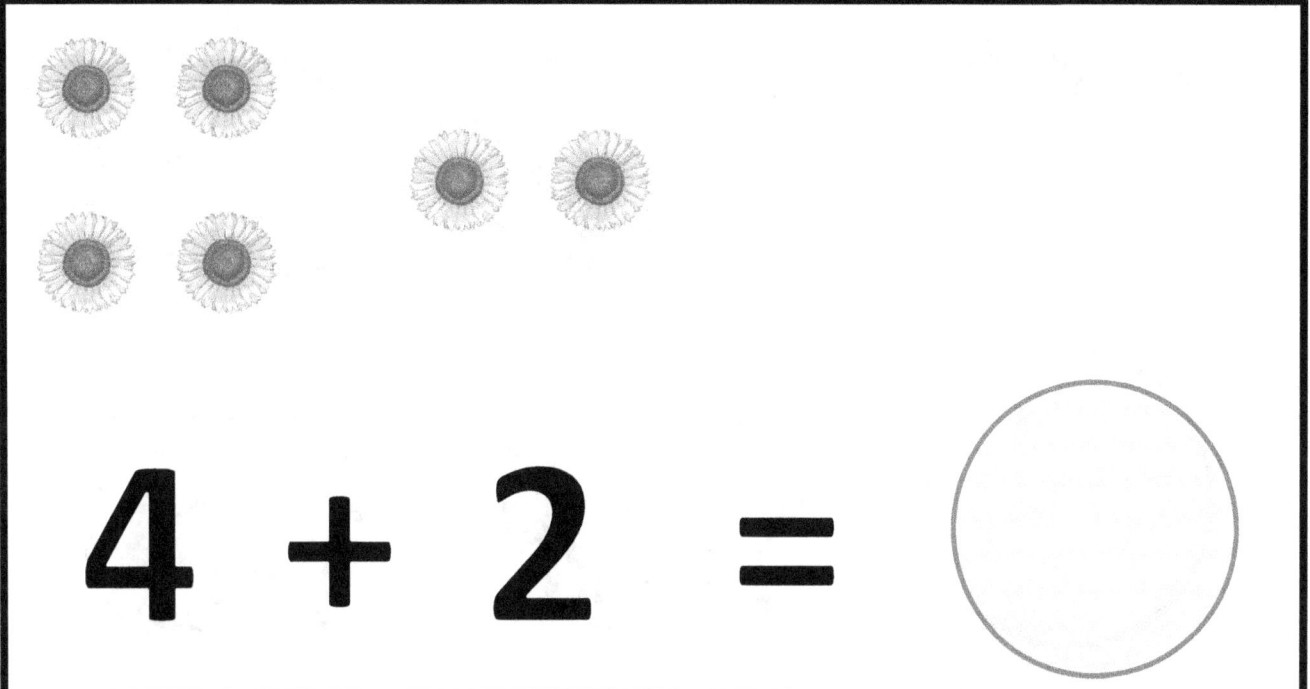

4 + 2 =

FIND MORE CAKES TO MAKE 6.

Make 6

FIND MORE TO MAKE 6.

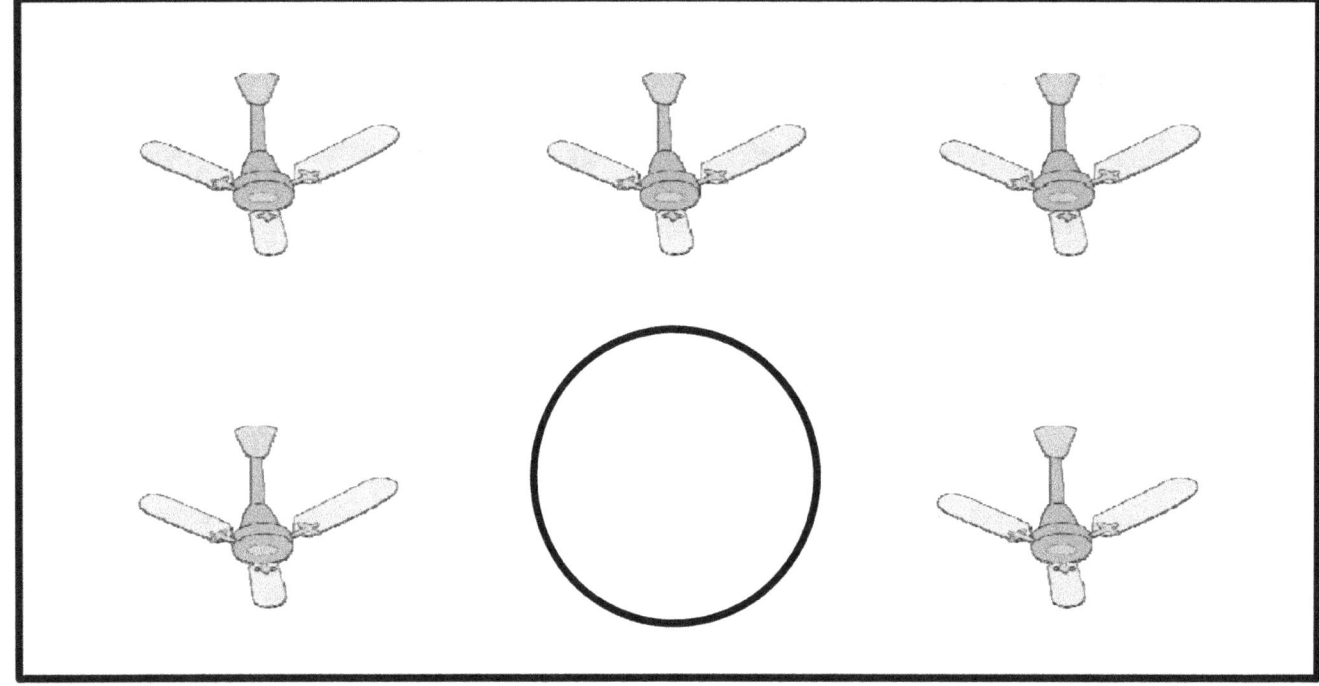

ADD SMALL GROUPS

ADD 1 MORE TO EACH GROUP.

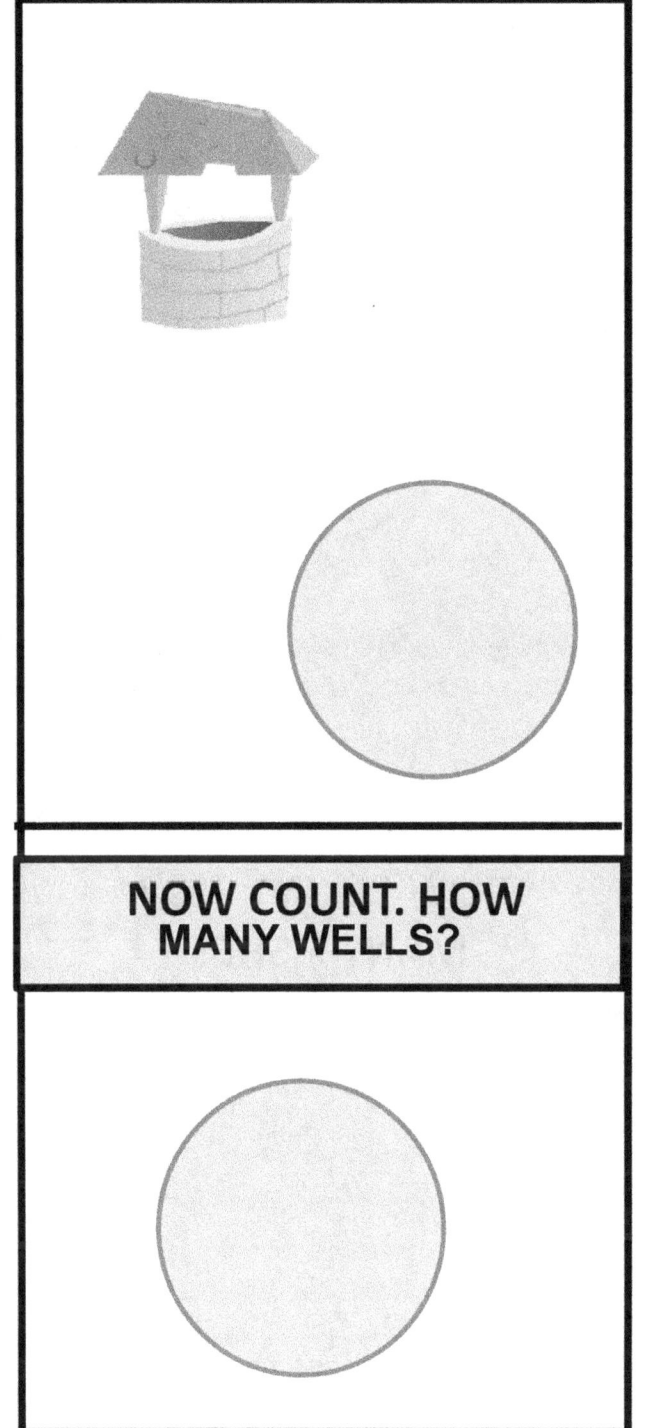

NOW COUNT. HOW MANY WELLS?

NOW COUNT. HOW MANY ZEBRAS?

www.nolathenurse.com

ADD SMALL GROUPS

ADD 1 MORE TO EACH GROUP.

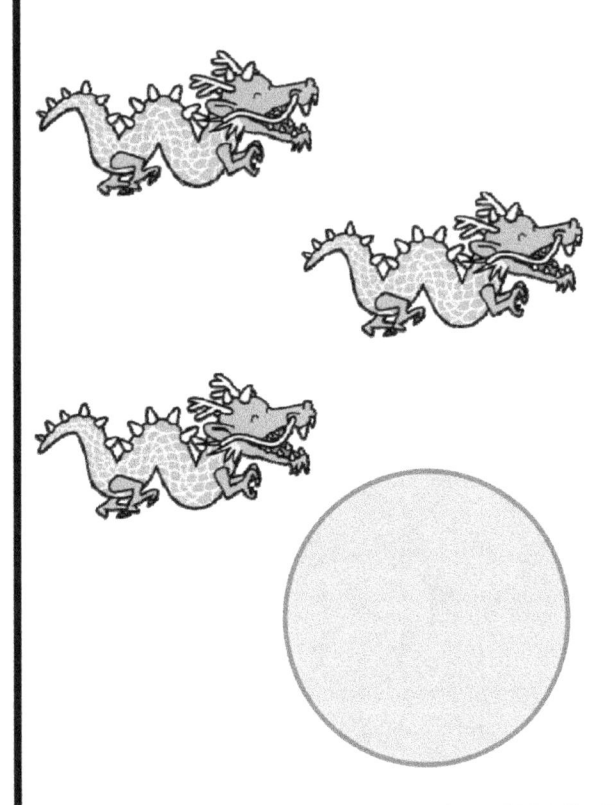

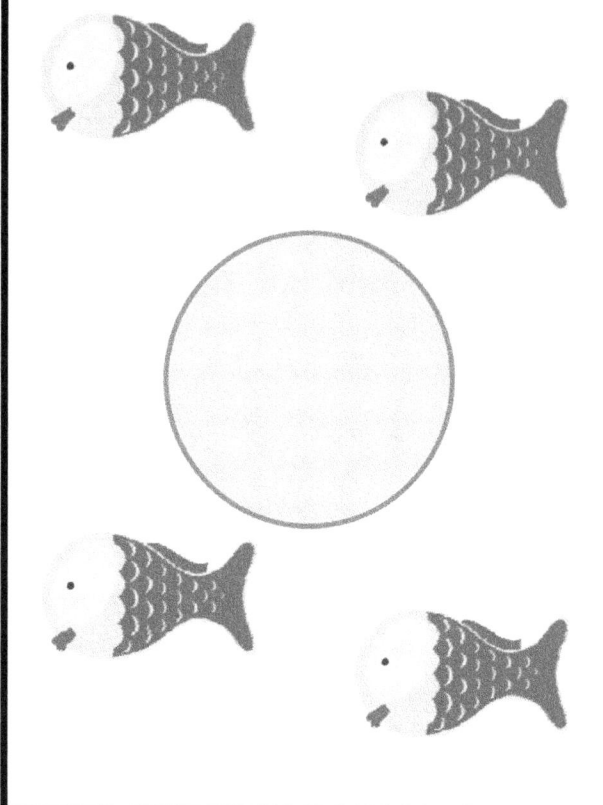

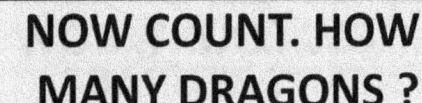
NOW COUNT. HOW MANY DRAGONS ?

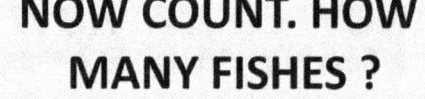
NOW COUNT. HOW MANY FISHES ?

www.nolathenurse.com

ADD SMALL GROUPS

ADD 1 MORE TO EACH GROUP.

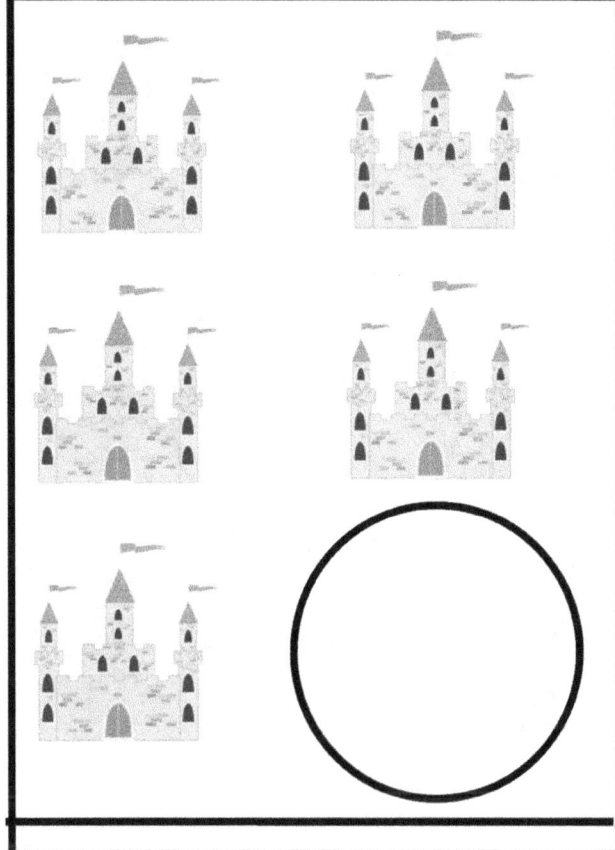

NOW COUNT. HOW MANY CASTLES?

NOW COUNT. HOW MANY ROOSTERS?

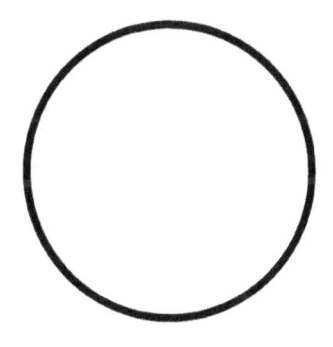

ADD SMALL GROUPS

ADD 1 MORE TO EACH GROUP.

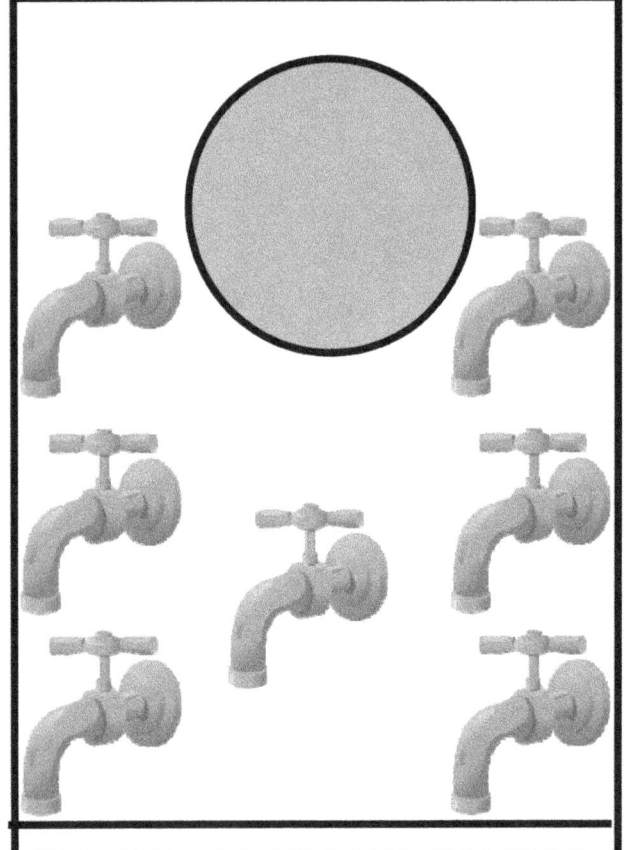

| NOW COUNT. HOW MANY TAPS ? | NOW COUNT. HOW MANY PRINCESSES? |

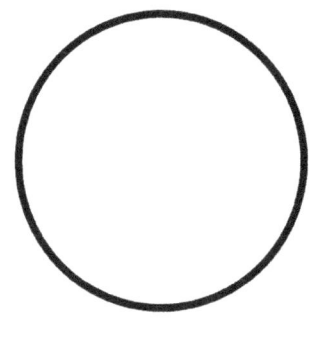

www.nolathenurse.com

NUMBERS

CUT & PASTE FOR WORKSHEETS 3 - 6

4　6

5

7

9　2

www.nolathenurse.com

NUMBERS

CUT & PASTE FOR WORKSHEETS 7 - 8

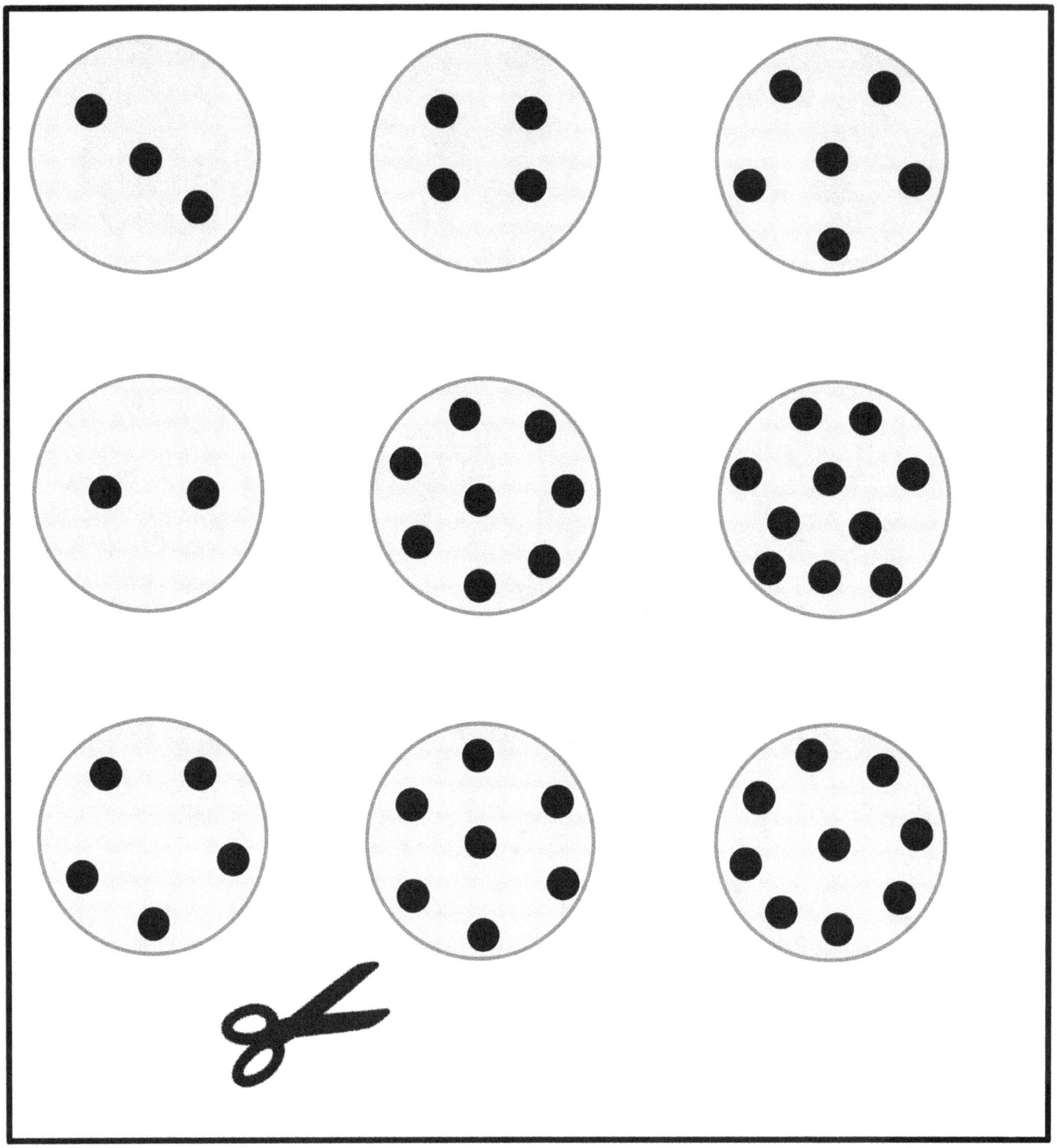

www.nolathenurse.com

NUMBERS

CUT & PASTE FOR WORKSHEETS 9 - 13

6　　3

8

5　　5

4　　4

3　　3

www.nolathenurse.com

NUMBERS

CUT & PASTE FOR WORKSHEETS 14 - 18

6

8 9

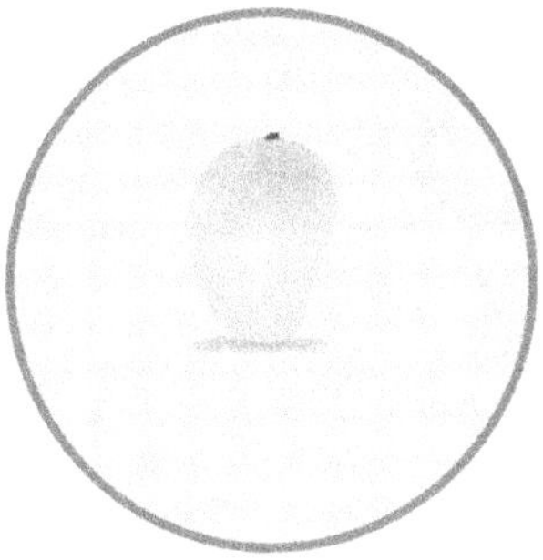

9 10

www.nolathenurse.com

NUMBERS

CUT & PASTE FOR WORKSHEETS 14 - 18

☂   🐐   7

5   7   6

✂   8

www.nolathenurse.com

NUMBERS

CUT & PASTE FOR WORKSHEETS 20 - 22

2

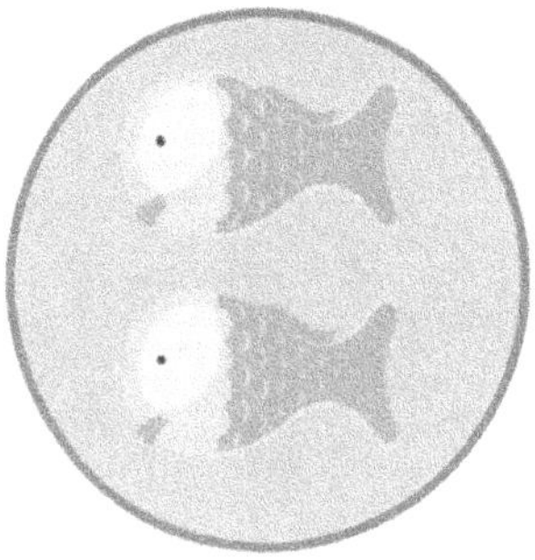

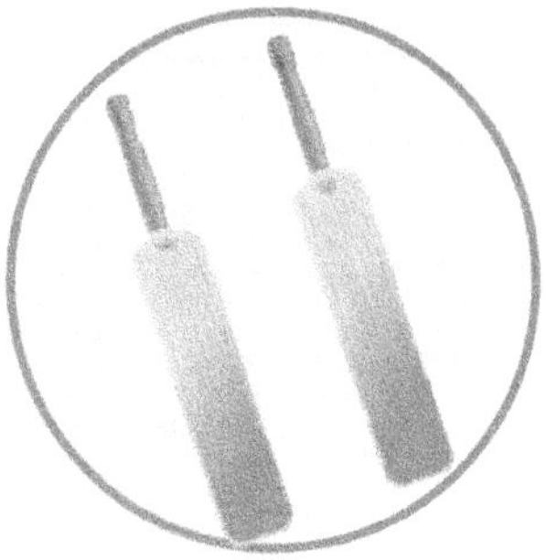

7

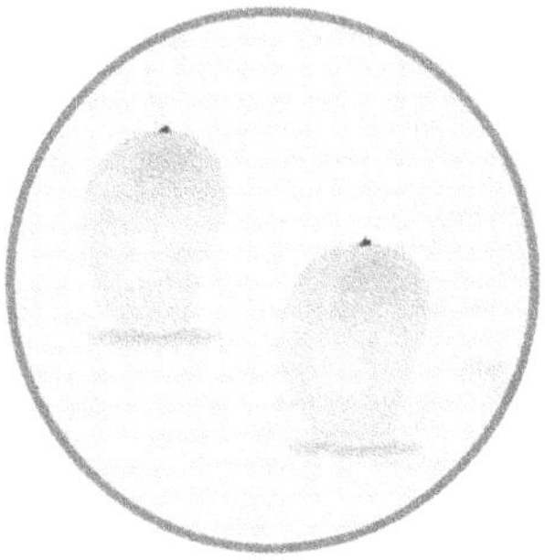

8   10

5   3

NUMBERS

CUT & PASTE FOR WORKSHEETS 23 - 28

www.nolathenurse.com

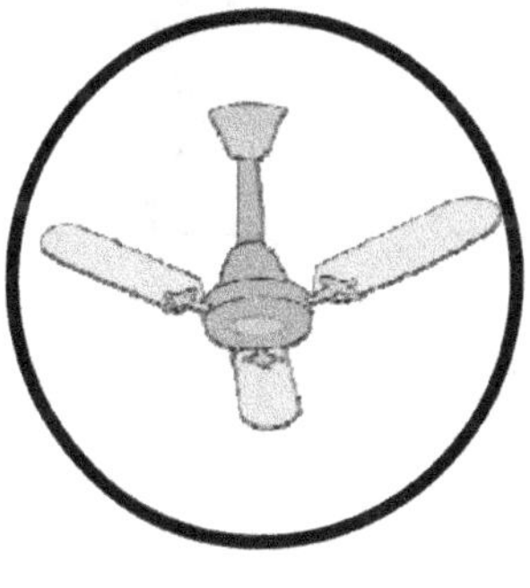

NUMBERS

CUT & PASTE FOR WORKSHEETS 29 - 32

www.nolathenurse.com

These following free color sheets are placed here to help you get to know the characters from the Nola The Nurse® children's book series. Enjoy and pick up a copy of the hottest selling children's book in America that was recently featured on The Harry Show!

Dr. Eden Nurse Practitioner

Anita

Gumbo

Dr. Baker Nurse Practitioner

Maddi the Midwife

More books by Dr. Baker

Nola The Nurse® She's On The Go Series Vol 1
Nola The Nurse® & Friends Explore The Holi Fest She's On The Go Series Vol 2
Nola The Nurse® & Friends Explore The Holi Fest She's On The Go Series Vol 2 Coloring Book
Nola The Nurse® Remembers Hurricane Katrina Special Edition
Nola The Nurse® Remembers Hurricane Katrina Special Edition Coloring Book
Black Dot
Nola The Nurse® English/Sight Worksheets for Kindergarten Vol 4
Nola The Nurse® Math Worksheets for Kindergarten Vol 3
Nola The Nurse® Activity Book for Kindergarten Vol 2
Nola The Nurse® Preschool Activity Book Vol 1
Nola The Nurse® Math/English Worksheets for Preschoolers Vol 5
Nola The Nurse® Math Worksheets for First Graders Vol 6

Upcoming Titles:

Nola The Nurse® STEM Activity Book for 5-8 year olds Vol 7

www.NolaTheNurse.com
DrBaker@NolaTheNurse.com

About the Author

Dr. Scharmaine L. Baker, NP is a nationally recognized and award-winning nurse practitioner in New Orleans, Louisiana. She has received numerous honors and awards for her contributions to healthcare in New Orleans since she became a family nurse practitioner in 2000, including the 2013 Healthcare Hero award (New Orleans City Business magazine) and 2008 Entrepreneur of the Year award (ADVANCE for Nurse Practitioner magazine).

Dr. Baker has a doctor of nursing practice (DNP) degree from Chatham University in Pittsburgh, PA, and she is a fellow of the American Association of Nurse Practitioners (AANP). She was inspired to make house calls while caring for her grandmother, who was ill and needed an in-home doctor.

After Hurricane Katrina, Dr. Baker was instrumental in caring for the sick and disabled in New Orleans, where hospitals had closed and doctors had evacuated but never returned. Her patient load went from 100 to 500 in only three months. Thanks to her passion and unwavering dedication to caring for homebound patients in her home town, Dr. Baker's story was featured on the CBS Evening News with Katie Couric.

Today, Dr. Baker maintains a busy private practice in New Orleans by making house calls to the elderly and disabled who would otherwise not receive healthcare.

When this award-winning and nationally known nurse practitioner is not on the road delivering keynote speeches and attending various other media events, she loves reading to her children, Skylar Rose and Wyatt Shane.

www.DrBakerNP.com
www.NolaTheNurse.com
https://shop.nolathenurse.com

www.ingramcontent.com/pod-product-compliance
Lightning Source LLC
Chambersburg PA
CBHW081356080526
44588CB00016B/2514